Lawrence Welk: The Life and Legacy of the Famous Bandleader and Television Host

By Charles River Editors

Lawrence Welk and Norma Zimmer in 1961

About Charles River Editors

Charles River Editors provides superior editing and original writing services across the digital publishing industry, with the expertise to create digital content for publishers across a vast range of subject matter. In addition to providing original digital content for third party publishers, we also republish civilization's greatest literary works, bringing them to new generations of readers via ebooks.

Sign up here to receive updates about free books as we publish them, and visit Our Kindle Author Page to browse today's free promotions and our most recently published Kindle titles.

Introduction

"Dreams do come true, even for someone who couldn't speak English and never had a music lesson or much of an education." – Lawrence Welk

Modern society has always been outwardly conscious of America's multicultural population, but an underlying misperception persists that the shaping of the new continent was overseen by a predominantly British presence. As a haven from despotic foreign governments and ceaseless wars that swept across Europe and back again, the archetypal American in fact originated from plenty of places, and this was made quite clear during the 20th century. World War I and World War II left a diverse American society clamoring for a grip on all its most intimate points of nostalgia, and while Europe sought the same solace in its state of ruin, the vast ethnic patchwork of uprooted immigrants from western and central Europe, Russia, and Asia found itself far from home, language, family, and familiar modes of expression in America, as did African Americans. Instinctively, people yearned for different forms of ethnic music.

By the mid-20th century, a musical revolution was stirring, and a generation that had not fought in the wars was ready to put the sorrows of the previous 50 years away. Requiring a commentary on modern life all its own, the first post-war generation went for self-expressed rock & roll, with Elvis Presley leading the movement. Jazz, incubated within America, grew into an increasingly sophisticated harmonic and rhythmic language, even though older generations were not able or willing to so easily follow. Not only did the elders' personal brand of music soothe the wounds of war, but the music reflected the dynamism of a scattered people's personality, ideals, and customs. From the trains of Woodie Guthrie to the fields of the Russian peasants, each story of suffering, distance, and celebration was played and sung in its own way.

For Scandinavians, central Europeans and Russians, the music of the homeland was a language as powerful as that which was spoken in the household. Such emblematic music and social dance functions held the family's national identity together and accompanied acts of faith in every spiritual tradition from the old world. By the time each immigrant group bonded to its distant history, virtually hundreds of distinct musical art forms found their geographical voice in North America, with few possessing much understanding of the other. Each brought the dances and songs from their home region, including the displaced African Americans. Some were overtly passionate, others decorous and refined, but all suited a perfectly crafted remembrance of familiar folk from one's birthplace. The Carter family sang of the poor life in the eastern mountains of America, while the Andrews Sisters elicited the war experience for returning American servicemen.

One immigrant son above all others took the step of defying the family farming tradition to participate in his people's musical remembrance. Lawrence Welk, born in 1903 in Strasburg, North Dakota, dedicated his life's work to fostering the sounds and steps of a family with its origins in Odessa, Ukraine, and the Alsace-Lorraine region. He began with the unwavering idea that providing uncomplicated and powerfully nostalgic music to members of his heritage would attract a devoted national audience in sympathy with Upper Midwestern ideals. He went on to craft a media culture based on Old World manners and decorum that endured for several decades. Known and loved by the parents and grandparents of the post-war generation, Welk remained impervious to the eye-rolling and mockery from young people and devotees of "sassier" musical fare. Shouldering his accordion, the national instrument of the Russian German presence in the United States, he never attempted to amass a universal audience, but instead held firm to a sliver of like-minded listeners and viewers.

Welk brought forms of European operetta, waltzes, polkas, and schottisches from the German and Austrian stage as well. Many Americans failed to realize that such forms had already saturated America, from the sentimental Irish arias of Victor Herbert in the early 20th century to the transplanted Viennese waltzes of Oklahoma and Carousel, courtesy of Rodgers and Hammerstein. The elements of German band music followed immigrants to the American Midwest and held a special social significance. Public band performances, hints of which are to be found in the finale of Beethoven's Ninth Symphony's commentary on class equality, represented a rare opportunity for non-aristocrats. In the public parks of the old country, they could stand next to their wealthy, titled counterparts to listen on equal footing.

Along the way, Welk became far more than a musician. He all but reinvented himself in later years as the host of *The Lawrence Welk Show*, which helped showcase up-and-coming musicians of different stripes in the second half of the 20th century.

Lawrence Welk: The Life and Legacy of the Famous Bandleader and Television Host profiles how he became the king of "champagne music." Along with pictures of important people, places, and events, you will learn about Miller like never before.

Old and New Worlds

"Music was my joy, my home, the one place I felt happy and secure." – Lawrence Welk

The community of Strasburg represented the epitome of the insulated immigrant as a German hamlet on the American prairie. Established by the railroad in 1902, it was named for Strasburg, Ukraine, from which the entire German population had been expelled. That town of the Russian Empire was in turn named for Strasbourg of the Alsace-Lorraine region ceded by the French to Germany in the late 19th century.

Welk's grandparents, Moritz and Magdalena Welk, are said to have emigrated from the region of Alsace-Lorraine in 1808, landing in the Ukrainian city of Odessa. In the late 19th century, Welk's parents, Christina Schwahni and Ludwig Welk, emigrated to North Dakota, some say from the German-French region of Alsace. Such is the common perception, but an elderly resident of Strasburg affectionately known as Uncle Pius claims that the migration was from the opposite direction. Generally regarded as the most knowledgeable of the town's citizens, he asserts that the magazines have it wrong, and that Welk's parents made the journey from Odessa.

Whichever is the case, the devoted Roman Catholic ethnic German couple arrived impoverished, with virtually nothing to their names. Their first year in the harsh northern environment was spent living in an upturned wagon covered with sod. North Dakota had only recently been admitted as a state and was for the Russian Germans considered a land of opportunity. Lawrence was to be born the sixth of eight children, speaking German at home and in exceptional times some primitive English. He later claimed to have begun the study of English in his 20s, but family members refute such an idea, attesting that he had early studies in school, with little success. Indeed, Welk dropped out of school in the fourth grade, and older residents recalled that it was because the boy was stricken with a ruptured appendix in 1913, a condition that was "usually fatal"[1] in those years. Strasburg had no hospital, and the nearest one was in Bismarck 80 miles away. Swathed in blankets, Welk was taken there on the wooden floor of a horse-drawn wagon and remained bedridden for a full year, never to go back to school.

Once he was mobile and healthy again, Welk began to work the modest family farm, and it was long assumed he would follow in his father's footsteps as a farmer. In such a culture, to continue in the profession of one's father was assumed, and for some time, Ludwig and Christina did not see the early signs of a break. For Lawrence to play the accordion for social occasions as his father had was also traditional, but at the time, considering music as a profession bordered on lunacy. Nonetheless, the young Welk dreamed of performing for large crowds as an accordionist even though he knew nothing of the musician's life or the ways of navigating the outside world. The first manifestation of his obsession appeared with his construction of a rudimentary violin,

---

[1] Maurice Condon, Germans from Russia, GRHC Heritage Collection, History & Culture, In Strasburg, They Remember Lawrence Welk When He Was the Leader of the Hotsy Totsy Boys.

employing a box and horsehair.

Ludwig had brought an antique accordion with him across the Atlantic, and taught accordion. Officially, no one else was to touch the instrument, but Lawrence played it regularly while his mother looked the other way. Eventually, the antique instrument wore out. One of Welk's uncles later claimed that Welk eventually secured another instrument for $15 by trapping muskrat, beaver, and badger, but this accordion soon became unsatisfactory as well.

Eventually, Welk's eyes fell upon a "rhine-stone studded"[2] catalogue instrument, and from that moment none other would do. He struck a deal with his father, one that the patriarch never believed would come to pass - if his son vowed to continue working on the farm to the age of 21, Ludwig would purchase a new instrument for him. After his 21st birthday, the young man was then free to leave as he wished. The new accordion allegedly cost the then enormous sum of $200, and some claim twice that amount. Either way, it was the equivalent of several thousand in the present day, a considerable extravagance for a Dakota farmer, and the young Welk astonished his father by paying back the sum in two years. When asked about the level of Welk's accordion playing, his Uncle Pius exclaimed, "You should have heard his father!"[3]

For years, Ludwig played a full regimen of weddings, parties, and other social occasions, "playing as long as there was anyone left to dance."[4] From the age of 13, Lawrence did the same, and many subsequently remembered the young man dressed for the stage riding off with the accordion in its sack at the rear, like a musical Johnny Appleseed. The band he eventually formed underwent several name changes, starting with The Biggest Little Band in America and changing frequently depending on the sponsor and increasingly prestigious affiliations. Other attempts to supplement his travel fund for touring were less successful, such as working as a restauranteur. His creation of the "squeezeburger," cooked on an accordion-shaped grill, never caught on as he believed it would.

Not yet able to be choosy in his affiliations, Welk and his initial band spent a time touring as part of George T. Kelly's vaudeville troupe, the Peerless Entertainers. Despite being billed as "the greatest accordionist in the world,"[5] he also posted handbills, sold candy between acts, and filled in for mute acting parts, since his thick accent was nearly unintelligible. One he recalled vividly was the part of a "Spanish corpse"[6] in a comedic murder sketch.

In the world of popular music, formal credentials were not necessarily a requirement, but Welk's attendance and 1927 graduation from the McPhail Centre for Music in Minneapolis added a nice touch to his on-air personality. A regional conservatory that to this day offers

---

[2] Maurice Condon

[3] Maurice Condon

[4] Maurice Condon

[5] WNAX, Radio 570, WNAX History-www.wnax.com'wnax-history/

[6] WNAX

education by instrument and age group, along with a regimen of music theory, the school has always boasted a talented faculty with regularly scheduled concerts in the Twin Cities.

When the Peerless Entertainers folded, Welk teamed with drummer Johnny Higgins, saxophonist Howard Kieser, and pianist Art Beal. In addition to the dance music and simple song forms of European and Russian cultures, Welk enjoyed an equally intimate love of jazz. In 1928, he recorded four "sides" for Gennett Records of Richmond, Indiana. Among the selections was a number never to be found in the vintage dance music of the radio, entitled *Spiked Beer*. One of the sides was eventually rejected.

Later sessions would appear in publication through Paramount Records in Grafton, Wisconsin, where Welk and the band recorded eight sides. Like Gennett, Paramount had been founded only a few years before and was an early home for Louis Armstrong, Hoagy Carmichael, Charley Patton, Jelly Roll Morton, and the famous "singing cowboy," Gene Autry. Welk's band was classified as one of the "sweet bands,"[7] as opposed to the "hot bands" of Duke Ellington and Benny Goodman, which ventured farther out to the borders of wild and virtuosic programming.

Jelly Roll Morton

With radio still too undeveloped to offer an entire career's worth of income, and wedding and dance tours taking up a tremendous share of performance work, Welk was seldom able to play jazz. For the band members, who were all advanced and virtuosic players, the wedding and dance pieces, typically designed for uncomplicated dance rhythms, did little for artistic creativity. Feeling they were stuck in a professional rut and unlikely to improve, the entire band quit, marking one of Welk's lowest moments. They explained to him that he would never become a success in the music business. As it turned out, the evolution of radio and television would prove them wrong over the following decades.

---

[7] Benson, Kit, Benson, Morgan, Lawrence Welk, Find a Grave.com – www.findagrave.com/memorial/1547/lawrence-welk

In an effort to avoid the Midwestern climate during the winter months, the reassembled ensemble resolved to head south to New Orleans, where music was more daring, diverse, and where the temperature was warm. At one point, all were too tired to continue driving and reached the nearest town to stop for the night. Learning that they were musicians, the residents of Yankton, South Dakota directed them to the single room studio of WNAX Radio. Welk arrived in town with enough for train fare south and three $1 bills pinned to the inside of his suit jacket. The band had played weddings over a wide area and were regionally known. Welk had even spent some performing time with a children's band, the Jazzy Junior Five.

E.O. Walgren, President of Schwenk-Barth Brewing Company and E.C. Madson, early radio man, had obtained a license to set up a "sending station"[8] under the call letters WNAX two years prior. None other than President Herbert Hoover agreed. A primitive station was set up on the second floor of the Wagner Block on the west side of Third and Fourth streets, and an aerial antenna was strung between two pipes on the top of the building. The little station broadcast at a maximum 50 watts, which is quite puny for a modern facility, but the signal was sent to 500 receivers, covering a 40-mile radius around Yankton. The broadcasts originated from a "talking machine"[9] for the 50th anniversary of the First National Bank, and the first radio concert was broadcast between 10:30 and 11:45 in the evening.

The radio was an exciting feature of the town, but it was too "new and untested"[10] for a steady supply of sponsors. Entering into a deal with an Iowa station, the studio came to occupy the third floor of a seed house, which was then selling Gurney seeds and trees. Welk and his band were to guarantee the station's success in short order. On the first day of his arrival came a meeting with station manager Chad Gurney. A hastily assembled audition resulted in a live broadcast one hour later, with a meal in between to keep the famished band members on their feet. In one evening, The Biggest Little Band in America was reborn on the public airwaves, soon to become known as the Lawrence Welk Novelty Orchestra.

The first contract for the Lawrence Welk Novelty Orchestra offered one week of appearances, but Welk secured an ongoing spot on WNAX programming. The band was alternately redubbed the Hotsy Totsy Boys, but when a new sponsor took over, they became the Honolulu Fruit Gum Orchestra. Other commercials interspersed between Welk's sets included Master Liquid Hog Tonic, and during these periods, calls came in requesting Welk's band for dance engagements. At the station, Honolulu Fruit Gum dominated, and Welk joined in the company spirit by stuffing his pockets with the product and handing it out to anyone who passed by.

Among the most important individuals who "passed by" was Fern Renner, a student nurse visiting the radio station with a group of colleagues. Upon catching first sight of her, Welk was

------

[8] WNAX
[9] WNAX
[10] WNAX

smitten, and in a desperate attempt to see her again, he braved an entirely bogus tonsil operation in the hopes that she would attend him during his recuperation. He was ultimately disappointed when someone else was assigned to the room, but she did visit him there when possible. Another account claims that the two met as a result of a real gallbladder attack, but that has since been disproven.

His relationship with Fern developed slowly, as one might expect from the couple's cultural origins. However, once she had completed her first studies, a position at St. Paul's Hospital of Dallas, Texas took her away. Undaunted, Welk and Renner mounted a prolific letter writing campaign. Finally, while engaged at the Broadmoor Club in Denver, Welk sent her an invitation to join him in Colorado, and she accepted. There, he convinced her to marry him in short order. In a barren Catholic church, the two were joined by two attendants from Yankton while Father Leo McCoy "nervously conducted"[11] the ceremony.

Although Yankton continued to serve as the couple's headquarters for the following 12 years, many engagements were still out on the road, and for that purpose, Welk acquired a specially designed sleeper bus, which the couple claimed resembled a "cattle carrier."[12] Prominent members of the band included Leo Fortin, Terry George, and Jerry Burke. When at home, the odd bus became a local landmark at the Deep Rock gas station.

Making It Bigger

"The William Penn Hotel in Pittsburgh... was the place where Champagne Music was born." – Lawrence Welk

Despite his duties at the radio station, a regimen of engagements around the country continued, and it was at a hotel in Pittsburgh that the image of champagne became associated with the Welk brand, by virtue of an innocent remark. One of the dancers cheerily exclaimed that the music was as "bright and bubbly as champagne,"[13] and the quip was doubly emphasized by the presence of a functional bubble machine left over from a movie premiere over a decade earlier. Welk, savvy to a fault for anything with which to raise the band's fortunes, borrowed both the bubble machine and the slogan. They served as the perfect foil for the forgotten audience Welk was sure still existed in between all the new movements of musical and dance styles.

The rules of his niche in the music market were clear. The music must be understandable and never overly embellished. The melody was to remain in the forefront at all times, with accompanying chords to be played the way the composers wrote them. The content avoided all elements of suggestiveness, and a distinguishable, reliable beat was to be always present for the simple dance steps enjoyed by his immigrant audiences. That listenership in turn brought along

---

[11] WNAX

[12] WNAX

[13] Find a Grave.com, Lawrence Welk – www.findagrave.com/memorial/1547/Lawrence-Welk

its American counterpart, an older audience from a war-torn, traditional, and decorum-bound culture seeking nostalgia and a sense of distant and courtly romance.

Welk and his orchestra upgraded the WNAX listenership to the point that he was able to extend his original one-week contract into a permanent position, performing daily from 1927-1936. However, sensing the need for a next step, Welk and his family moved to Omaha, Nebraska, Fern's hometown, and following the Yankton years, the band fell into the habit of driving thousands of miles for one-night events. At home, he could only manage an occasional performance at the Chermot Ballroom or Joe Malec's Peony Park Amusement Center. This could not sustain a family, and the long-distance trips began to wear on the marriage.

Initially, Welk's new manager Vic Schroeder, who specialized in booking bands through the Midwest, cautioned him to remain in Omaha. Finding a steady spot in one of the Omaha clubs was, Welk believed, the way toward a happier life at home. Their home in Yankton sold almost immediately, and Welk was soon ready to begin, until he discovered that he was severely restricted without an Omaha Musician's Union card. Visiting the union office, he was instructed to wait for a period of six months. Questioning Schroeder on this disappointing reality, the manager expressed shock that his client had not known the ropes well enough in his own city. Within a week, Welk had returned to long distance performing, and he was at this point tempted to wash his hands of the entire idea of music as a profession.

In an aesthetic sense, Welk enjoyed the touring life, and he had compiled an extraordinary list of friends and acquaintances in every direction. Band members groaned as they crossed the Midwest and endured watching Welk point out house after house and identifying each family. At one point, they called his bluff, so he turned into the next driveway and greeted Harry Kerstein, who was milking his cow near Hooper, Nebraska. Naturally, the band was invited to stay for breakfast, and in the end they stayed through dinner as well.

Eventually, touring became unworkable, so Welk and his wife tried their hand at chicken farming. Fern maintained that they might have made a real success of it if not for the fact her husband invited everyone and their brother home for free chicken dinners and sent each one home with a free chicken. Within six months, Welk was again in the music union's offices, and this time he was informed that no vacancies existed at that time. As Schroeder explained, most of the union officials were musicians as well, and to have Welk on the list would cost them work. His credentials were well-known, and many artists in the region were threatened by his presence in the city.

The couple prepared to move once again, but Welk was hesitant to sever all connections. He purchased the house at 8009 Miami from Edgar and Ellen M. Wegand in July of 1936 for $6,500. Decades later, he was to sell it to the Laugel family for "$2 and other valuable considerations."[14]

The eventual destination was the city of Chicago, thanks in large part to a prestigious hall and the opportunity of a career breakthrough if Welk could land it. The Trianon Ballroom was hailed by many as "the most beautiful in the world."[15] So prestigious was the new facility that its opening during the "Roaring 20s" was heralded in by George Gershwin's colleague Paul Whiteman and his New York Orchestra. Procuring a spot at the Trianon spelled the end of touring by car and scavenging for the odd engagement here and there with limited funds.

Whiteman

The Trianon was owned and operated by Greek immigrants Andrew and William Karzas. The two had already succeeded with prestigious restaurants, a nickelodeon, and movie theaters, but their two ballrooms, the Trianon and the Aragon in Woodlawn and Uptown, were by far their greatest moneymakers. The giant Trianon opened at 62nd and Cottage Grove. Designed by Rapp

[14] Lawrence Welk, Brief Omaha History – www.allaboutomaha.com/Omaha/Lawrence-Welk.php

[15] John Morris, Chicago Patterns.com/Trianon "World's Most Beautiful" – www.-chicagopatterns.com/trianon-worlds-most-beautiful-ballroom/

& Rapp, who had overseen several of Chicago's most notable landmarks, Trianon was designated as an elite "major society gala" with a "no jazz"[16] policy, including floor spotters to police the crowd's decorum. Despite its targeted refinement, Trianon was a favorite venue among the white lower middle classes and the working youth, as the mystique of the enormous ballroom evoked a sense of luxuriousness for those inhabitants of the city who were entirely unaccustomed to it. Social dancing was a mainstay of entertainment in the era, and the goal had been to create the largest dance floor in the world. By its inauguration, the space was 170 feet long and 50 feet at the top height. Of particular interest to Welk was that the Trianon housed its own radio station. The call letters, WMBB, signified "World's Most Beautiful Ballroom."

Little time was required for Welk and his orchestra to gain renown in Chicago, instilling the confidence with which to move his family, including a son and two daughters, and to stay for 10 years. In a considerable uptick of demands on his professional time, Fern remained "the rock of the family."[17] One description of the couple suggested that whenever Welk threatened to be swept away with a big head, it was Fern that could "straighten it out."[18]

Such temptation was certainly present, as Welk repeatedly drew crowds of thousands in a space able to hold 1,500 dancing couples. On the side, he recorded with Vocalion Records in New York City, a label acquired by Brunswick records two decades before, one that featured many early African American greats. In 1941, Welk recorded for Decca as well, venturing out of his familiar public genre. The labels of Mercury and Coral were soon added. During this period, he collaborated with Red Foley on a version of "Shame on You," written by Spade Cooley. Such collaborations formed the secret life of Welk's career. Foley, a smooth baritone, was a pioneer of crossover into country, western swing, sacred music, honky-tonk, and gospel. Cooley, a fellow bandleader, was admired as a country fiddler until his arrest and conviction for the murder of his second wife, Ella Mae Evans.

---

[16] John Morris

[17] Closer Weekly Staff, Lawrence Welk's Family Reveals the Beloved Hollywood Star 'Didn't Care About Fame, Closer Weekly –
www.closerweekly.com/posts/lawrence-welks-family-says-he-never-forgot-his-roots-exclusive/

[18] Closer Weekly

Foley

Such opportunities added to Welk's regular fare and were the result of fortunate timing. The 1940s proved to be a period in which the accordion became the national instrument in many areas, and for the major record labels of the time, including Decca, Columbia and Victor, accordion recordings were published in enormous quantities. On one New York City station, the instrument was featured on a daily basis, and celebrity artists such as accordionist Charles Nunzio recalled playing as many as 35 performances per week. Ethnic radio spots for European immigrant music were everywhere, reflecting the sounds of central Europe. The city of Milwaukee boasted 36 accordion schools, and one of the many schools in Minneapolis listed 17 accordion teachers on its payroll. Sales of accordions were massive nationally, and the distinctive sound became a favorite "amateur leisure pursuit."[19] At the height of it, there was the face of a smiling Lawrence Welk on the cover of virtually everything having to do with the instrument. He was far from the most accomplished player in the business, but he symbolized the spirit of the immigrant story behind the music.

One difficulty had dogged Welk's immigrant culture since his teens, and it again became a sore point thanks to Senator Joseph McCarthy from Wisconsin. The infamous communist hunter first took his seat in the Senate four years before *The Lawrence Welk Show* was conceived, and he was in full "black list" mode through much of the musician's later success. Through the Russian-

---

[19] Marion Jacobsen, Squeeze This, A Cultural History of the Accordion in America, Chapter Three, Squeezebox Rock, 2012, *Folklore Studies in a Multicultural World*, University of Illinois Press.

Ukraine migration of his family, and as a member of the Russian-German farm culture, Welk and others were obligated to tamp down that association throughout the early stages of the Cold War. Among McCarthy's primary targets was academia, allegedly harboring a national, covert communist movement. With the patriotic warmth emitted by Welk and his cast, few audience members were aware of his national heritage. Along with most of the Russian-German contingent in America, he adopted a demeanor exhibiting his people's "unassuming ways and lack of college education."[20] Welk's home culture of rural North Dakota was actually one of multiple threads of the migration. His own people viewed the accordion and European social dancing as a high level of entertainment, where the Russian Germans of Nebraska, Kansas, and Colorado viewed it less intimately. In those regions, accordion worship gave way to the "Hackbrett," or hammered dulcimer. With less cultural affinity, Welk had to win over the southern and western immigrants through the same charm that brought the rest of America into the fold.

   With his national radio show reaping high ratings throughout the 1940s, the prestigious venues kept coming when Welk took over the summers at the Roosevelt Hotel in Midtown Manhattan. The giant palace, housing two grand ballrooms, was named for Theodore Roosevelt and was the chosen venue for Guy Lombardo's New Year broadcasts for 30 years. Welk took over for Lombardo when Lombardo took his band to Long Island every summer. Like the Trianon in Chicago, the giant New York hotel with 1,025 rooms housed its own radio station, WRNY. During the golden decade of the accordion, the Welk band made a number of what were referred to as "soundies," a prototypical example of the modern music video. From 1949 through the following two years, Welk was sponsored by Miller High Life, the "champagne of bottled beer,"[21] a fitting affiliation.

---

[20] Timothy J. Kloberdanz

[21] Find A Grave.com, Lawrence Welk

Lombardo

The Lawrence Welk Show

"By 1969, when I celebrated 45 years in the music business, I also had 45 people in our musical family." – Lawrence Welk

Around the 1950s, it became clear that the best days of the Welk phenomenon in the Windy City were behind him. The big band craze of the '30s and '40s was on the wane, never to return other than as a nostalgia genre, and Welk's once immense crowds were thinning out. The Trianon manager saw it coming before the band did, refusing all requests for raises. Not content to wait for the collapse, Welk finally packed up the band and set on tour once more across the country.

Welk promoter Sam Lutz began to correspond with KTLA Television by mid-tour. KTLA was a prominent local station in Los Angeles, but early TV experienced the same difficulties with sponsors as had early radio stations like WNAX. Lutz began to pester the manager of the station to put Welk and his band on camera, and after weeks of Lutz's efforts wore them down, KTLA agreed. However, there were to be no open arms or red-carpet walks; the manager refused to pay any portion of Welk's expenses to reach Los Angeles, in fact requiring $300 from the band in order to defray shooting costs. Welk and the band were to appear without pay as well.

Welk had never thought to test the television experience and had many concerns shared by most making the transition from radio to TV. However, he accepted the barebones offer and made his local TV debut on May 2, 1951. By this time, the ensemble had become the resident orchestra at the Aragon Ballroom in Pacific Ocean Park, located in the Santa Monica area but only a few miles from Hollywood, Brentwood, and Bel Air. Situated on Lick's Pier, the Aragon was built in 1922, serving much the same function as the Trianon, although less formal. It later reopened as a discotheque, the Cheetah Club.

The Lawrence Welk Show, created by Klaus Landsberg, was born at the Aragon. Fresh off its Chicago success, the band, now known as the Champagne Music Makers, had reached a high level of fame, and Welk was able to parlay a six-week engagement into a permanent spot that spanned several years, regularly playing to nightly crowds of 7,000. Meanwhile, KTLA soon began to broadcast live on a weekly basis. Despite the vastly different medium, the result was identical to the days in Yankton and Chicago, with numerous calls and letters coming from the area begging for more. The surprised station manager gave the band an entire week, with a minimal amount of pay, and in a brief period, the show attracted the interest of the Dodge Motor Company, on the prowl for a program to sponsor. Welk rejected them outright at first, due to the fact his group was already under a sponsorship arrangement with Chevrolet. However, Dodge persisted, and a new contract was signed one month later. Welk began his first permanent show with high ratings at a time when Dodge experienced an upsurge in business.

With new confidence in the trajectory of their sales figures, the automobile manufacturer took the next big step by offering Welk his first national, "coast-to-coast"[22] weekly show. Four years after the band's unheralded arrival to a local Los Angeles station, the American Broadcasting Corporation snatched the show up, presented its first national broadcast of *The Lawrence Welk Show*, and kept it in the forefront of programming for decades. Each member of the band received a new Dodge automobile except for Welk, who received a new model every year.

In the mid-1950s, Welk sensed that it was time to leave the Aragon, so he moved nearer to the center of the Los Angeles action. Expressing his regret at leaving the Santa Monica audience, he observed, "The Palladium will be a much more central location for the tremendous tourist trade we seem to attract."[23]

Three large components of the American audience were available, including the affluent, the young, and the middle-class elderly. The interests of the first two went off in different directions,

[22] Lane Sunwall, First Lawrence Welk Broadcast, Williston Herald, July 2, 2020 – www.willistonherald.com/community/first-lawrence-welk-broadcast/article_a3cb0f7a-bbd7a5-df6e7ecd73f9.html

[23] Lonny Lynn.com, Aragon Ballroom, Santa Monica, California – www.lonnylynn.com/Ballrooms/BRaragonCA.htm

but Welk specifically targeted the third, who were war-weary and not responsive to early rock &
roll, free-form dancing, and what they considered to be an unbecoming attitude among the
young. Dance and social behavior had always been for the older viewers both formalized and
heavily guarded against the off-color, rude, or obscene, as they understood it. Welk's first rule
was that those qualities would never be violated, even in the minutest detail. While the
requirements for modern success in television are more clear-cut in the modern day, no one at
that time was entirely certain what formula would encourage profits, high ratings, and good fan
mail. Added to the uncertainty, which opened the industry to massive experimentation, much of
the new medium was often performed before a live audience, a feat requiring an inordinate level
of confidence and quick reflexes.

That said, Welk knew precisely the type of Americans he sought: those he grew up with and
others who shared a similar worldview. He openly described himself as "square and proud of it."[24]
By the 1950s, several Midwestern men were on their way to stardom, including Nebraska
entertainer Johnny Carson and UCLA basketball coach John Wooden, the "Wizard of
Westwood," born in Indiana. Welk counted both men among his friends, but while Carson
forsook his roots for the life of a slick and worldly L.A. celebrity, Welk followed the same path
Wooden did. In essence, rather than creating a new paradigm in either leadership or the arts, both
men turned to home to preserve an existing tradition.

---

[24] John Miller, From the Great Plains to L.A.: The Intersecting Paths of Lawrence Welk and Johnny Carson, *The Virginia Quarterly*: Vol. 179
No. 2 (Spring 2003), University of Virginia

Carson in 1957

Just as movie actors had struggled with the transition to sound, Welk had his share of discomfort becoming a visual image in front of what was previously his radio audience. Usually fluent and relaxed before a live audience, he was reined in by cue cards because speaking itself was a career-long issue. Welk claimed to not have spoken English for the first time until his 20s and felt burdened by a thick European accent, but as is often the case, viewers and promoters found such an accent to be a plus. Some who knew him maintain that he even though he studied English in his early school years, he never outgrew an awkward style of speech since he only spoke German at home. Researcher John Miller asserted that fellow performers found him "numb with shyness"[25] despite having considerable flair among his own. Having dropped out of grade school, Welk preferred to let the music speak for itself, but show business relied on sight as well as sound, and Welk is said to have once been urged to speak between numbers by the manager of a Milwaukee club. When the bandleader replied that he was "no good at it," he was informed that the pay would be higher. Before a live audience, his comfort grew to a point where he came to enjoy it, but the constrictions of television always remained daunting.

---

[25] John Miller, Virginia Quarterly

The format of *The Lawrence Welk Show*, which debuted in 1951 and premiered nationally four years later, was carefully assembled on a certain type of entertainment frequently mocked as "quaint" by more modern genres. Welk's goal was not to elicit anything approaching a riotous response in the audience, but to produce a soothing satisfaction, a transport to other times and locales. The mindset was described by Sinclair Lewis as a form of "measured merriment that preserves respectful intentions, inhibiting pruderies, the operating platitudes, and the residual wistfulness"[26] of one's imagination. Enamored of his community of fellow "squares," Welk would not give an inch to the modern California style. The bedrock of the show's allure was to consist of "clean fun, understandable music, pretty…wholesome girls…entertainment that builds up and doesn't tear down."

The weekly offerings were formalized as well. Welk understood one unchanging reality from his era – that listeners and viewers are particularly drawn to couples and ensembles, regardless of how thrilling they might find the solo performer. The smattering of two-person intimacy was ever-present in both dance and song. Comedians were entirely absent from the programming as they were difficult to police in terms of off-color content. Behind it all was the famous band, and every installment began with Welk posing before his ensemble, carrying the extra-large baton common to bands of the era. A remnant of earlier times where classical orchestra conductors employed them, the full-length rod banged on the floor had long since disappeared from history. In Welk's case, the band only required the conductor to initiate the action as they were advanced and small enough to stay together through the simple arrangements. For classical conductors, the beat is ongoing, and the supple push and pull of the musical phrase with large ensembles is considerably more difficult. The European dance forms played by Welk required the opposite, a beat that was never bent.

Welk's catchy method of starting a piece with "a Vun and a Two"[27] became a national catch phrase that has endured long after the maestro's death. So, too, is his congratulatory pronouncement at the end of many numbers: "Wunnerful, Wunnerful!" Ironically, it is a phrase that he long denied ever saying. Despite the presence of an assistant leader, Myron Floren, who as a rule played as a virtuoso accordionist, Welk reserved one spot in each show for himself to play, either as a soloist or in duets. The champagne theme was ubiquitous, and the bubble machine was always on call to erupt sporadically throughout the show. As a finale, Welk always danced off the credits with the "champagne lady," an ongoing fulltime position usually filled by one of the show's performers. *The Lawrence Welk Show* aired faithfully at 9:00 pm EST. Through part of the 1950s, he headlined two such ABC productions, the other on Monday from 1956-1959. That production was eventually moved to Wednesday and retitled *The Plymouth Show*. Unlike much of early television, large segments of Welk's primary show were pre-recorded, either the day before or on broadcast day. With such a format, too many things could go wrong in an entirely live setting. Performances were evenly divided between lip and finger-

---

[26] John Miller, Virginia Quarterly

[27] History.com

synching. Most of the numbers were recorded in famous Hollywood studios.

Specialty acts came and went through the years, but a core group became intimately associated with the show depending on the strength of the fan mail. Among the most central ensembles of the show were the Lennon Sisters, who spent much of their career associated with Welk. Without a doubt, the sisters were the most famous of the singers ever to appear over the show's long run.

Dianne, fondly known as Dee Dee, was the oldest at 16 years of age. Peggy was born two years later, and Kathy was 12. Janet was the youngest, made her first appearance at nine years of age. They went on to a 60-year career with various replacements along the way by various sisters and quartet children, and they sang for seven different presidents. It's somewhat surprising that Welk could hold on to them for such a long period, considering that he paid the famous quartet by union scale. It is said that he professionally adopted them from their debut at the Christmas Show in 1955. They maintained an advertising relationship with the Welk resorts, and they eventually found a new home singing at the Welk Theater and the Andy Williams Moon River Theater in Branson, Missouri.

Pictures of the Lennon Sisters

Alice Lon undertook multiple roles with the show, but she was primarily known as the "Champagne Lady" who danced the finale with Welk himself. The relationship came to a bad end and demonstrated how much of a stubborn taskmaster Welk could be in his pursuit of a totally pristine environment. On a particular evening, he fired Lon for showing too much leg, although an alternate story claims that she crossed her legs. He declared that his show would harbor no such "cheesecake images,"[28] odd since generations of female cellists had once been instructed to do just that. The fan mail, however, was brutal against Lon's firing, and in a rare reversal, he attempted to rehire her, to no avail. The position was taken by regular performer Norma Zimmer.

---

[28] Maria Sonevytsky, The Accordion and Ethnic Whiteness: Toward a New Critical Organology, *The World of Music*, Vol. 50 No. 3, Accordion Culture, Verlag für Wissenschaft und Bildung

Welk with Alice Lon on *The Lawrence Welk Show*

Even the Lennons, above reproach in Welk's mind, struggled with a desire for more sophisticated popular music and a looser look, but kept their own counsel over the matter. They, too, were called on the carpet on one occasion when seen in one-piece bathing suits for an Escondido Resort ad. The mail that flooded the office was generally livid, and he pronounced the results to the sisters with a trumpeted "I told you!"[29]

The Lawrence Welk Show struck it rich when Joe Feeney, famed for his rendition of *Danny Boy* and other nostalgic songs for tenor, introduced Jo Ann Castle to the bandleader. Jo Ann Zering offstage, the native of Bakersfield, California borrowed a stage name from an accordion manufacturer. Singing by the age of three, she was on stage with Tex Williams and Spade Cooley at 13 as an extraordinarily virtuosic "honky tonk" and "boogie-woogie" piano player. Welk promoted her as the "Queen of the Honky Tonk Piano," and she could ably shoulder an accordion if needed.

---

[29] Tom Gorman, Staff Writer, Los Angeles Times, May 19, 1992, Lawrence Welk Obituary – www.latimes.com/local, obituaries/la-me-lawrence-welk-1992-20519-20160516-snap-story.html

Welk with Castle (left) and Cissy King

Despite lasting for years on the show, Castle eventually became entangled in legal disputes and accusations that ran counter to everything Welk espoused. Taking the "no-nonsense personality" to extremes, she was prone to alcohol-induced fist fights. From her hiring four years after the show's debut, she was allegedly complicit in cases of child molestation, drugs, and alcohol, in time losing guardianship of her children. Her career would resurface years later in Branson and other Welk tributes.

Feeney himself occupied a specific type of lyric tenor voice, often called the "Irish tenor" in the mode of Irish great John McCormack. Such a voice type was popular before and after the years of World War II, a staple of the opera world. A regular for many years on the Welk Show, the Nebraskan Feeney supported a family of 10 children. He sang until his death at 76.

Tap dancer Arthur Duncan, among the only African American performers to appear with Welk, was spotted by manager Sam Lutz. Originally intending to study pharmacy at Pasadena State College, he was curious to "see what this show business thing is all about."[30] In time, he appeared with celebrities such as Red Skelton and Jerry Lewis, and extensively toured the major cities of Europe and the Middle East. Among his most eye-catching moments on *The Lawrence*

---

[30] Arthur Duncan, Tap Dancer (1966-1982), Welkshow.com – www.welkshow.com/duncan/html

Welk Show was a tap routine on a piano top, in which he made use of the sideways slide toward the precipice while somehow avoiding disaster. The smoothness of his footwork created the appearance that he was dancing on a slippery waxed surface.

Duncan

Welk's second-in-command was Myron Floren, a "consummate musician"[31] and advanced accordionist capable of crossing over into difficult classical repertoire with ease. Affiliated with Welk from the beginning and remaining with him for 30 years, he was known to take the baton when the bandleader was needed elsewhere. Floren's daughter helped write his autobiography, *Accordion Man*, in which he was said to have handled Welk's road manager duties. From the farm community of Roslyn, South Dakota, Floren and Welk shared a sympathetic relationship that seemed to remain untroubled by rivalry. The bandmaster dubbed him as "The Happy Norwegian." Floren had already appeared regularly on the radio show, *Major Bowes Amateur Hour,* and transitioned to television with a charming ease. Among his most memorable moments

[31] Faithe Deffner, In Memory of Myron Floren, Accordion.com – www.accordion.com/memorials/mem/floren-myron/index.shtml

for Welk audiences was a virtuosic rendition of "Lady of Spain."

Despite his ability to tackle a piece of any difficulty, Floren supplemented Welk's success by wholeheartedly embracing his credo: "Play what they want to hear, and they will always listen."[32] For Polish audiences, a barrage of mazurkas was at the ready, along with polkas and schottisches for Swedes and Norwegians. Even with Floren's gifts, for Welk to play on every show remained an important gesture, as something of the Dakota farm boy was said to come through his playing. Floren was described by one afficionado as possessing more of a "conservatory than cornball"[33] style. Still, as time went by, the bandleader played somewhat less often. The affinity of Welk and Floren endured. In a later interview, Floren fondly recalls looking out over a crowd of 21,000 at Madison Square Garden as Welk observed, "Isn't it wonderful what can happen in this country to a couple of farmers from the Dakotas?"[34]

In the mid-1950s, Welk was able to score another heavy hitter in clarinetist Pete Fountain of jazz and Dixieland fame. A star of The Tonight Show Band as well with Johnny Carson, he began as a teen in the jazz district of New Orleans on the advice of a doctor that the clarinet might help with a "respiratory ailment."[35] He later opened his own club on Bourbon Street. For a time, Fountain toured with trumpeter Al Hirt and the Dukes of Dixieland before joining *The Lawrence Welk Show*. All was well until Christmas two years later, when he jazzed up a version of "Silver Bells." After leaving the show, his only observation was an impression that "champagne and bourbon don't mix."[36]

The bowed strings component of *The Lawrence Welk Show* was more than ably led by concert violinist Dick Kesner from Sioux City, Iowa. A conservatory musician before joining the Freddie Martin band in the pre-television age, he first appeared with Welk two years into the Aragon period, before the show went national. Welk was "so enamored"[37] with Kesner's virtuosity that he bought the new star a Stradivarius. Nevertheless, Kesner left the show after six years to record more music and increase his regimen of live concerts. He died of a heart attack soon after in California while driving his car.

Buddy Merrill of Torey, Utah stayed with Welk as one of the show's finest guitarists beginning in 1955. Born Leslie Merrill Behunin, he joined the show in the year ABC picked it up. Playing both acoustic and steel guitar, he had a youthful energy in his performing, making him "very popular with the ladies."[38] Respected throughout the industry, he stayed with the show almost to the end of the decade when he was drafted by the Army. Upon his return three years later,

---

[32] Faithe Deffner

[33] Marion Jacobsen

[34] Faithe Deffner

[35] Welk Show.com, Pete Fountain, Clarinet (1957-1959) – www.welkshow.com/fountain.html

[36] Welk Show.com, Pete Fountain

[37] Welk Show.com, Dick Kesner, Violin (1953-1959) – www.welkshow.com/Kesner.html

[38] Last.fm, Buddy Merrill Biography – www.lastfm/music/Buddy+Merrill/+wiki

Merrill formed an extraordinary guitar duo on the show with Neil Levang. They stayed together for the following 12 years.

Fearful as Welk was of comedians, he was equally hesitant to work with married couples and the inherent danger of a relationship going wrong at the worst possible time. Only one couple was ever engaged for the show, Ralna English and Guy Hovis. Ralna was a country and gospel singer with a great deal of career experience. As a sideline, she provided for herself by making commercials. She met Hovis at The Horn in Santa Monica, where they both worked. On the Lawrence Welk stage, they were the perfect picture of blissful domesticity, a cardboard cut-out of well-ordered, contented '50s living. Still, as Ralna later explained that however much they may have been in love, the two "never really liked each other."[39] Backstage tensions may have been present to a higher degree than with other performers. The duo singing act depended largely on Ralna's skill and archetypal country voice. Guy possessed a high baritone to tenor instrument that was passably attractive, with a quick vibrato that matched his wife's voice well. The marriage did not last, and they ceased performing together for some years.

As performers reflected back on Welk's rigorous rehearsal schedule and intensity, it is clear that in the forefront of the bandleader's mind was not just the name of the artist. A performer who did not fit in was cast away as easily as a mediocre one, but of greatest importance was that the show "aggressively enforced the inoffensive."[40] To those who were forced to cultivate the upper Midwestern immigrant experience rather than flow from it, Welk reflected an idealized artistic purity that either no longer existed or may never have existed at all. In the local dance hall, things were just what they were, and people did what fun-loving people do. However, for Welk, every pre-packaged and pristine moment shown to the national audience was a symbol to fend off the tide of modern music and the breakdown of formal social dancing. He made the accordion broadly visible in a way that would have been impossible for other instruments. It was a form of accompaniment one could buy without breaking the bank, and it could be mastered at a basic level. One could not do the same by emulating Jascha Heifetz, arguably the greatest violinist of the century, who played a Stradivarius.

The story of the immigrant overcoming the language barrier to become the "beloved American entertainer"[41] was skillfully woven into the visual language of the Welk empire with few daring moments to interrupt the tautness of the vision. Recent music was seldom performed, and what pieces there were had been sanitized of all harmonic roughness and rhythmic wildness. One exception occurred in December 1956 when the show performed a satirical version entitled "Nuttin' for Christmas," now a popular old chestnut. Sometime later, the Lennon Sisters again collaborated with Norma Zimmer in "The Wah-Watusi." Such exceptions seem insignificant through a modern lens, but the change puts the constraints on the show's performers in

---

[39] The Famous People, Lawrence Welk – www.thefamouspeople.com/profiles/lawrence-welk-3296.php
[40] Marion Jacobsen
[41] Marion Jacobsen

perspective.

By the end of the 1950s, *The Lawrence Welk Show* had begun as a summer replacement called the *Dodge Dancing Party*. However, as *The Lawrence Welk Show*, it was already such a strong part of the television scene that satirists swept in like vultures to poke fun at its obsolete language and rules of decorum. Critics, knowing precisely what they were to see without actually spending the time to attend, gave full vent to their self-gratuitous humor. Frank Rasky, Canadian journalist and Entertainment Editor of the *Jewish News*, declared that the Welk phenomenon "was the squarest music this side of Euclid."[42] Satirist Stan Freburg, who popularly trafficked in almost vaudevillian lampoons on the day's events and most prominent individuals from early American history to the present, went to great lengths for Welk. He mocked the band with a carefully assembled group of fine players. Billy May, composer, arranger, and trumpeter, took on the spoken role of Welk, overemphasizing a pattern of stumbling words. An unseen character dances on Welk's accordion until it is shattered to bits. In the end, the bubble machine runs amok, and the entire Aragon Ballroom floats out to sea amidst the wailing of discordant accordion music. The skit is rife with exclamations of "Wunnerful, Wunnerful!"

Welk, ordinarily dismissive of such mockery, was not amused. When he and Freburg met, he again denied having ever uttered such a term, yet it would be the title of his autobiography years later. Although he would certainly not have admitted it, changes were made in Welk's programming. He played fewer accordion solos as he felt the guitar relegated his culture's instrument to obsolescence. He increased the appearance of new music, if only by a small percentage. Careful not to lose anyone from the core audience, he flirted with sanitized arrangements of The Beatles, Burt Bacharach, Neil Sedaka, The Everly Brothers, and others. Among the first was a rearrangement of Presley's "Don't be Cruel."

Before the change, Welk enjoyed his parallel musical passions elsewhere and largely in secret. In 1959, he signed with Dot Records. A savvy investor, he joined in the production business by creating labels of his own, such as Vanguard and Sugar Hill. Both he sold to the Concord Bicycle Music Group, but kept the Ranwood label on which he had recorded himself. Ranwood was eventually licensed to Concord for a period of ten years.

The satirists barely noticed the show's continuing evolution or Welk's parallel skills. Critics from across the country reacted resentfully to the pillars of his wholesome culture. One labeled the entire enterprise as "Ham hock philosophy…chock full of nothing."[43] Another referred to the television "bauble," likening *The Lawrence Welk Show* to "Rotarian entertainment."[44] On some level, it appealed to a few of the less cynical old guard who saw Welk as "a moralist, a rustic sage, but above all a missionary."[45]

---

[42] Geni, Lawrence Welk – www.geni./people/Lawrence-Welk/6000000019795471628

[43] John E. Miller, Journal of American Studies

[44] Marion Jacobsen

[45] John E. Miller

To the middle-aged and elderly base who would miss any event other than the show, any blow struck against the tsunami of rock music was a righteous one. Devotees believed that a Midwestern ethic was the intended norm for the national psyche, and that all else was a psychopathic distortion of the American mission. The Midwest was "the most American part of America,"[46] as much as the South believed that their region was the most faithful. The art form of Midwestern music was "friendlier, less snobbish, more sanguine."[47] In a tangible sense, immigrant expression in dance music and instrumental excellence with the accordion demonstrated "a greater confidence in Democracy than the east,"[48] according to Indiana novelist Meredith Nicholson.

The persistent assaults aside, *The Lawrence Welk Show* went on its way with no discernable dip in the ratings or enthusiasm expressed in the fan mail. The singers and dancers were as beloved as ever, and the band enjoyed success with instrumental hits as well. A cover of "Yellow Bird" was well-received, having already established familiarity through Harry Belafonte and the Kingston Trio. "Calcutta" was the most successful instrumental of Welk's career. Originally a German pop song entitled "Tivoli Melody," it went through several changes before arriving at its final title in 1961, recorded by Dot Records. Uncharacteristic devices accompanied the accordion and harpsichord with more boisterous rhythms and punctuated hand clapping. Welk himself was fairly apathetic toward the song, but Music Director George Cates was sure of its success, and he insisted. Welk deferred, astonished that Cates had such a belief in it.

---

[46] John E. Miller, Journal of American Studies
[47] John E. Miller, Journal of American Studies
[48] John E. Miller, Journal of American Studies

Welk in 1960

The state of North Dakota honored its native son in 1961 by bestowing on him the Theodore Roosevelt Rough Rider Award as its charter recipient. Such awards and patriotic reverence for the presidency was an immovable pillar of Strasburg thinking. The only occasion on which Welk and his cast missed a performance in three decades occurred due to the assassination of President Kennedy.

As rock music became more pervasive in the 1960s, Welk turned to innovative slants on programming that would change the pace without changing the purity. In 1966, a series of shows featured music, art, and stereotypical demonstrations of costume for various nations around the globe. Among the most popular was the Italian tribute, featuring the usual stars with forced accents surrounded with the appearance of an opera cast and stage. Hosted by dancer Bobby Burgess, one of Disney's original Mouseketeers, the now grown child star danced the *Tarantella* with Barbara Boylan, and the Blenders sang "Finiculi Finicula." Marimbist Jack Imel led the cast in *Carnival of Venice* with a gaily clad Jo Ann Castle and the Lennon Sisters. Pianist Bob Ralson played the "Isle of Capri," and Aladdin Pallante sang "That's Amore." Dick Dale sang and played the clarinet in "Vieni Su" (Come South).

Thematic episodes continued, and a 1970 Special Thanksgiving broadcast entitled *Thank You America* was a delight to Russian Germans who had grown weary of hearing about injustice perpetrated by the Soviet Union. Welk was invited to become a member of the American Historical Society of Germans from Russia. Such an invitation brought up once more the danger of being too strongly identified with the Soviet Union. He politely slithered away from the matter by politely declining. His explanation evoked the beliefs of his father, who "taught us to forget the old country and become Americans."[49]

Individual stars fell away from time to time to give full vent to their musical creativity. Others groaned under the burden of the show's musical simplicity. Players who were considered giants in the outer musical world kept themselves under wraps during the Welk tapings, playing arrangements that were for them playable by children. Singers yearned to sing jazz, rock, and other forms. The bandleader, however, would not budge. The man who had grown up at the hands of Ursuline nuns still believed that his choice of music and its pristine expression, was "a course in right living."[50] He treated his musical family as his own father had treated his, with all the discipline and expectations of high behavior, and with character placed above skill. Despite some exceptions, some of which Welk regretted, the bulk of his performers were brought from the Midwest, from the same background as his own. Singers, normally brought from Hollywood references, big city talent agencies and resumés built on shows from Los Angeles and New York stages, came instead from Midwestern church choirs. For those who remained with Welk through the years, the rural Christian backgrounds by which they had been raised were not stifling, but comforting.[51]

As for the more cosmopolitan members, Pete Fountain left amicably and barely spoke of the matter as his career continued without a hitch. However, Alice Lon, the dismissed "champagne lady," was the opposite of the Midwestern decorum rule. What galled Welk more than the issue itself is that she offered free gossip treats to reporters at will and sat for interviews filled with bitterness and scandalous tidbits, making his life's dream sound more like a daytime soap opera drama. What Lon had to say about Welk's microscopic control of the show's minutest components was true. He made every decision and seldom consulted anyone. Like his friend John Wooden, employees had to play "his brand of ball"[52] since he was the one who would take the fall if it failed.

---

49 Timothy J. Kloberdanz
50 John E. Miller
51 John E. Miller
52 John E. Miller

That said, with the exception of Stan Freburg's assault, Welk remained immune to alternate audiences partaking of the social revolutions of the 1960s. He was a person who could not be moved from the outside. Customs and styles of expression were things bound to change, but universal truths would not.

In 1965, Welk received an honorary doctorate from North Dakota State University. It was the sort of honor that one generally receives in their waning years, or at some time well past their major life accomplishments. Everything was changing around him, and from that environment, it must have seemed as if an anachronistic figure was finally getting his gold watch. However, anyone who thought so was gravely mistaken. Welk was able to go on for several more years, and even after *The Lawrence Welk Show* was thought to have vanished from the American scene altogether, he skillfully brought it into syndication nearly up to the 21st century.

In 1966, Welk recorded a jazz album on Ranwood with saxophonist Johnny Hodges, a proponent of the "other" sort of band, headlining with Duke Ellington. The album contained standards such as "Misty" and "Someone to Watch Over Me," but had a decidedly uncharacteristic tone. He had co-founded Ranwood with Randy Wood, formerly of Dot Records. The studio and label are still in business under the umbrella of the Welk Music Group. The two recovered ownership of everything Welk had ever recorded for Dot, all to be repackaged and sold through Ranwood. The content was manufactured by Teleklew Productions and leased back to Dot. Such an arrangement was not possible for the Coral Recordings, which were owned by Universal. Welk acquired Wood's interests in Ranwood in 1979, and in the 1980s, it was folded into the studio holdings with Vanguard and Sugar Hill.

Welk's Final Years

"I just wrote a book, but don't go out and buy it yet, because I don't think it's finished yet." – Lawrence Welk

The Lawrence Welk Show was finally dropped from ABC in 1971. However, Welk immediately moved it into independent syndication through 250 American and Canadian stations, entitled *Memories of Lawrence Welk*. Syndication did not signify an endless rebroadcast of past shows. A new cast was gathered into the studios to prepare new shows for touring with new stars.

Among the most memorable was one of the few ethnic performers hired since Arthur Duncan. Singer Anacani, with an attractive stage presence and sweet, soothing voice, joined the cast in 1973. The Mexican soprano's full name was Anacani Maria Consuelo y Castillo Lopez Cantor Montoya, but she was introduced on stage only as "Lovely little Anacani."[53] She employed Carmen Miranda-like moves in her numbers and quickly became an audience favorite. Anacani

---

[53] Welkshow.com, Anacani – www.welkshow.com/anacani.html

had first auditioned for Welk at his Escondido Resort, one of several he established in the later years. Her family had moved to the United States from Sinaloa, Mexico. She soon appeared in Welk's *Salute to Mexico*, another of his popular international offerings, singing "Luna." Anacani remained with Welk for nearly another decade. Even after her departure, she continued to tour with other Welk "family members" coast-to-coast. Among her typical venues have been Bearcreek Farms of Bryant, Indiana, the American Music Theatre of Lancaster, Pennsylvania, and Harrah's of Lake Tahoe. In addition, she has appeared with numerous symphony orchestras singing lighter classical repertoire and "pops" concerts. Each year, she has worked the annual telethon for the West Texas Rehabilitation Center in Abilene.

The idea of the sister trio or quartet was revived when the Semonski Sisters joined the cast in the '70s. They had enjoyed a breakthrough moment when Donald O'Connor arranged an audition for them. Musical skits were in fashion at that time, and they spent nearly three seasons performing them with Welk. The Semonskis were in turn replaced in 1977 by the Aldridge Sisters, a vocal duo act. Sheila and Sherry began as church and community artists and were both flight attendants. They joined the cast following schooling at Lubbock Christian College and West Texas State University. Welk auditioned them in Nashville despite having no openings at the time. He put them through three more sets of auditions before allowing them to appear as guest stars before filling in for an artist who resigned. Welk teamed them with Roger and David Otwell, the Otwell Twins, to create a two-couple feature. The sisters were also able guitarists.

Not able to keep the sort of schedule that he once had, Welk began to suffer more bloopers in the course of making shows, some of which he enjoyed immensely in later recollections. Among his favorites was an errant introduction of the Welk orchestra as "The Shampoo Music Makers," but he was clearly losing a little of his keen edge, and finances were not holding him back from taking things easy or retiring altogether. He had acquired vast real estate holdings and was considered one of the wealthiest men in the music and television business. Along the way, he purchased the royalty rights to over 2,000 songs, including the entire works of Jerome Kern.

The symbol of his onstage success, the accordion, was in a state of serious decline. Two decades before when ABC picked up *The Lawrence Welk Show*, 120,000 accordions had been sold, now replaced by the guitar. Vanity entered the American psychology about the appearance of performance. Men complained that accordions made them look fat, while guitars tended to create a sleek and worldly look. And, as the final death blow, men agreed that the accordion was a poor choice of instrument for meeting girls. Some blamed Welk himself for playing the instrument on screen too often. William Schimmel, a Juilliard School–trained composer and world-renowned accordionist, delivered an academic paper entitled *Learning from Lawrence Welk*. He suggests that Welk is in part responsible for "burdening the accordion with cultural baggage."[54] This, apart from the fact that the accordion had made Welk the second richest man in Hollywood next to Bob Hope.

---

[54] Maria Sonevytsky

Following the opening of his Resort and Country Club in Escondido, Welk established a second in Branson, Missouri. A late devotee to the game of golf, Welk began to enjoy appearing in the numerous celebrity golf tournaments such as the Bob Hope Classic, and the Bing Crosby International Classic. He took the time he had once lacked to play with friend John Wooden. True to form and ever the kitsch-loving entrepreneur, he constructed a golf cart that tooled around the course blowing bubbles. As always, he enjoyed swimming as well, but as a North Dakotan, swimming was never to be done outside. His production of books written in partnership with Bernice McGeehan increased with titles such as *Wunnerful, Wunnerful, My America, Your America*, and *Lawrence Welk's Musical Family Album*. A second autobiography emerged entitled *Ah-One and Ah-Two*, written in 1974.

Meanwhile, the original Welk artists from the show rejoined the enterprise in 1982. Many missed the old times and found a refreshing novelty in touring aboard a 40-passenger bus, playing 100 one-nighters per year. Jo Ann Castle had been gone from the show for 12 years, and declared that "It's like I never left."[55] Once paid by scale, the artists made more money in the retro-performances. Ralna English observed that although the audience saw Welk as "a fatherly type guy, he was the total boss."[56] She enjoyed the new attitude borne of having nothing left to prove – "We've eliminated bad attitudes. Gripes, complainers are out."[57] Castle cited Welk's professional personality on the set as entirely different than his demeanor off it. She asserts that "he seemed frozen reading cue cards…but man, that guy knew how to work a crowd."[58] The artists add that Welk was not particularly a generous man, paying stars by scale, and not prone to giving gifts. It was of note that as the core of his initial success, the band members made more money than the headliners. Most feel that by taking the time to work within Welk's image of the old world, they became aware of growing fossilized, with one noting, "The 60s passed us by, and it's been hard to catch up."[59]

At long last, Lawrence Welk retired from all phases of show business in 1992, at the age of 89. He died in Santa Monica at his home, dubbed The Champagne Towers, on May 17 of that year. His obituary reported that Welk died peacefully and was buried at Holy Cross Cemetery in Culver City of L.A. County. His epitaph reads, "Keep a Song in Your Heart."

The *L.A. Times* obituary referred to him as a "reluctant farm boy,"[60] not an innovator but "sweet and simple."[61] He never played a song that lasted more than three minutes, in case an audience didn't like it. He received little praise for television work or from great players

---

[55] Hugh Boulware, Lawrence Welk's Road Show, Chicago Tribune, May 26, 1988 – www.chicagotribune.com/news/ct-xmp,-1988-05-26-8801020491.html

[56] Hugh Boulware

[57] Hugh Boulware

[58] Hugh Boulware

[59] Hugh Boulware

[60] Tom Gorman, Staff Writer, Los Angeles Times, May 19, 1992, Lawrence Welk Obituary – www.latimes.com/local/obituaries/la-me-lawrence-welk-1992-20519-20160516-snap-story.html

[61] Tom Gorman

employed in the orchestra to "sublimate their abilities"[62] with Welk's arrangements. However, untold adulation poured from his audience, one he knew and understood. Performers agreed that Welk was "insightful toward his audience's wishes."[63] Forcing his brilliant musicians to play juvenile arrangements, likened to making the thoroughbred pull the milk wagon, they were forced to admit that in a tenuous profession, it was the steadiest job in town.

In 1993, North Dakota State University acquired an enormous bulk of the Lawrence Welk Collection to preserve and make available his music and memorabilia. This collection included 10,000 musical arrangements, multiple scrapbooks and manuscripts, photographs, artifacts, record albums, publications, and oral histories. The Elmira Brechtel collection containing correspondence from performers with the orchestra has been merged into one collection. The scrapbooks are fragile and have been photocopied. Some of the activities of the Norma Zimmer Fan Club are included, as are 695 albums and 8,700 song titles. In the same year, Welk was inducted into the International Polka Hall of Fame, and he received two stars on the Hollywood Walk of Fame, one on Hollywood Boulevard and a second for television on Vine. Despite such fame derived from a television show, Welk prized the live audience above all else. He once likened a road show to an "instant barometer,"[64] adding that "A quiet audience just kills me."[65] Still, he took immense pride in leading "the show that wouldn't go away."[66]

Through the sensitive lens of racism in the present day, Lawrence Welk's career would undoubtedly be perceived in a different way by a modern audience. In a question of whether his productions were racist, one might answer that it is not overtly or consciously so. He sold European music from regions with scant African cultural characteristics. Immigrants from the same areas came to the U.S. and reflected their cultures in the same way, hailing from a white church and white dance background. Only in jazz did the two influences meet.

Some assert that in the white folk culture of Lawrence Welk, a general "disdain"[67] for African musical characteristics was present. The goal, however, was to attain the cultural purity of central Europe's musical and dance expression, however idealized as it may have been. Whether it was overt racism, racism of omission, or merely a presentation of what one knew to the exclusion of all else is difficult to ascertain. Many musical cultures, including African American music, present undiluted examples of their own forms. Likewise, many African musical environments do not include the dance steps of others that play out as symbols of European colonialism.

For Maria Sonevytsky, the musical whiteness operates as a form of "otherness"[68] with the

---

[62] Tom Gorman

[63] Famous People.com

[64] Tom Gorman

[65] Tom Gorman

[66] Tom Gorman

[67] Marion Jacobsen

accordion as its symbol, but it is more associated with ethnic whiteness, not white and black conflict. It is, in her view, a white immigrant culture embedded with and devoted to pure memory of a distant mother country.

Some would suggest that Lawrence Welk should be enshrined among the greatest American success stories, alongside other entertainers like Bob Hope. Others believe that his life's work has been an exercise in tyrannical forms of "puritanism."[69] This credo requires a counterpart, a propagation of the belief that rock and other new forms of music are evil by nature. They represent to the immigrant gospel a new and dangerous American dream, especially when the guitar has "psychosexually"[70] replaced the accordion as the male American instrument. Since the days of Elvis Presley and The Beatles, Welk's music has gathered additional associations to various pockets of resentment in the American city, but the fondness for Welk's vision abides in a slice of the American demographic. In a documentary on Welk with Kathy Lennon as host, the response and fundraising pledges that came in were of such magnitude as to allow two years of reruns from the fruits of a single event.

In June 2019, *The New York Times Magazine* listed Welk among hundreds of artists whose materials were destroyed in a fire at Universal. Plenty were heartbroken by the news, and mmny loyal employees still work at the Welk Resorts as of 2020. Adriene Edwards comes to work each morning in Escondido and hugs Welk's statue before beginning the day. Edward's first hourly wage was $1, starting 40 years ago. Welk is counted among the vast majority of employees as having been "humble and kind." They remember the first Escondido facility, a modest motel with four rooms, and the new properties in Palm Springs, Tahoe, Branson, Breckenridge, Santa Fe, and Cabo San Lucas. Former employees of the band continue to play in Branson each year, and the Live Lawrence Welk Show still tours the U.S. and Canada during the year.

The town of Strasburg is still a "huddle of houses"[71] off North Dakota State Route 83. When entering the community, visitors will immediately notice signs to Welk Dam or to the Lawrence Welk Swimming Pool and Picnic Park. In the post office hangs Welk's portrait next to that of Lyndon B. Johnson. Similarly, Ludwig and Christiana Welk's homestead remains a tourist attraction in a town that boasts 549 people. The homestead covers 6.1 acres from a farm that originally boasted over 600. The house was built in 1899 of mudbrick, a common method of construction among Russian Germans, and surviving remnants include a summer kitchen, outhouse, blacksmith shop, granary, and a barn built around 1949. The farm originally grew wheat and other crops, raised chickens for eggs, cows for cream, and was family-run until 1965.

Whatever one's view on the North Dakota spirit that compelled Lawrence Welk to go out and make his own music, he is admired for his steely refusal to alter the scene at all. It seems as

---

[68] Maria Sonevytsky

[69] Maria Sonevytsky

[70] Maria Sonevytsky

though he followed a page from Alexis de Tocqueville: "Cultivate the arts that serve to render life easy in preference to those whose object it is to adorn it."[72] Welk condensed the sentiment into an uncomplicated credo: "If they can't hum it after we play it, it isn't for us."[73]

Online Resources

Other books about music by Charles River Editors

Further Reading

Benson, Kit, Benson, Morgan, Lawrence Welk, Find a Grave.com – www.findagrave.com/memorial/1547/lawrence-welk

Boulware, Hugh, Lawrence Welk's Road Show, Chicago Tribune, May 26, 1988 – www.chicagotribune.com/news/ct-xpm-1988-05-26-8801020491-html

Brainy Quote, Lawrence Welk – www.brainyquote.com/author/Lawrence-welk-quotes

CBS8, Lawrence Welk's Most Loyal Employee Celebrates 55 Ye4ars of Service – www.cbs8.com/article/news/local/zeverlyjones/lawrence-welks-most-loyal-employee-celebrates-55-years-of-service/509-9892dbf2-a759-41cd-b212-eacd7dff94c6

Closer Weekly, Lawrence Welk's Family Reveals the Beloved Hollywood Star 'Didn't Care About Fame' (Exclusive) January 21, 2019 – www.closerweekly.com/posts/larence-welks-family-says-he-never-forgive-his-roots-exclusive/

Condon, Maurice, Germans from Russia, GHRC Heritage Collection, History & Culture, In Strasburg, They Remember Lawrence Welk When He Was Leader of the Hotsy Totsy Boys – www.library.ndsu/grhc/history-culture/lawrence-welk/welktvguide.htm

Deffner, Faithe, In Memory of Myron Floren, Accordion.com – www.accordion.com/memorials/mem/floren_myron/inex.shtml

Encyclopaedia Britannica, Lawrence Welk, American Bandleader – www.britannica.com/biography/lawrence-welk

Geni, Lawrence Welk – www.geni.com/people/Lawrence-Welk/6000000019795471628

Gorman, Tom, Times Staff Writer, Los Angeles Times, May 19, 1992, Lawrence Welk Obituary – www.latimes.com/local/obituaries/la-me-lawrence-welk-1992-20519-20160516-snap-story.html

---

[72] John E. Miller, Virginia Quarterly

[73] Brainy Quote.com, Lawrence Welk – www.brainyquote.com/author/lawrence-welk-quotes

History, This Day in History/March 11, 1903, Lawrence Welk is Born - www.history.com/this-day-in-history/lawrence-welk-is-born

Huey, Steve, Lawrence Welk, AllMusic – www.allmusic.com/artist/lawrence-welk-mn00001168/biography

Jacobson, Marion, Squeeze This: A Cultural History of the Accordion in America, Chapter Three, Squeezebox Rock, 2012, *Folklore Studies in a Multicultural World*, University of Illinois Press

Kloberdanz, Timothy J., Symbols of German-Russian Ethnic Identity on the Northern Plains, *Great Plains Quarterly*, Vol. 8 No. 1 (Winter 1988) University of Nebraska Press

Last.fm, Buddy Merrill Biography – www.lastfm/music/Buddy+Merrill/+wiki

Lawrence Welk Show, Stars of the Lawrence Welk Show – www.welkshow.com

Lawrence Welk Show, Stars of the Lawrence Welk Show – www.welkshow.com/anacani.html

Lawrence Welk, Brief Omaha History – www.allaboutomaha.com/Omaha/Lawrencer-Werlk.php

Lonny Lynn.com, Aragon Ballroom, Santa Monica, California – www.lonnylynn.com/Ballrooms/BRaragonCA.htm

Miller, John. E., Lawrence Welk and John Wooden: Midwestern Small Town Boys Who Never Left Home, *Journal of American Studies,* Vol. 38, No. 1 (April, 2004) Cambridge University Press

Miller, John, From the Great Plains to L.A.: The Intersecting Paths of Lawrence Welk and Johnny Carson, *The Virginia Quarterly*, Vol. 79 No. 2 (Spring 2003) University of Virginia

Morris John, Trianon "World's Most Beautiful Ballroom", Chicago Patterns, July 25, 2014 – www.chicagopatterns.com/trianon-worlds-most-beautiful-ballroom/

NDSU Archives, Lawrence Welk – www.library.ndsu.edu/ndsuarchives/collections/lawrence-welk

National Enquirer, The Lawrence Welk Show Sex Scandals, Sept. 14, 2017 – www.nationalenquirer.com/photos/the-lawrence-welk-show-sex-scandals/

Richey, Dr. Lance, University of St. Francis, Fort Wayne, Indiana, Lawrence Welk and Catholic Business Ethics – www.legatus.org/lawrence-welk-and-catholic-business-ethics/

Sonevytsky, Maria, The Accordion and Ethnic Whiteness: Toward a New Critical Organology, *The World of Music*, Vol. 50 no. 3 Accordion Culture, Verlag für Wissenschaft und Bildung

State Historical Society of North Dakota, Welk Homestead State Historic Site – www.history.nd.gov/historicsites/welk/

Sun Signs, Lawrence Welk, TV Host - www.sunsigns.org/famousbirthdays/d/profile/lawrence-welk/

Sunwall, Lane, First Lawrence Welk Broadcast, Williston Herald, July 2, 2020 – www.willistonherald.com/community/first-lawrence-welk-broadcast/article-a3cb0f7a-bbd7a5-df6e7ecd73f9.html

The Famous People, Lawrence Welk – www.thefamouspeople.com/profiles/lawrence-welk-3296.php

Welk Show.com, Arthur Duncan, Tap Dancer (1966-1982) – www.welkshow.com/duncan.html

Welk Show.com, Pete Fountain, Clarinet (1957-1959) – www.welkshow.com/fountain.html

Welk Show.com, Dick Kesner, Violin (1953-1959) – www.welkshow.com/Kesner.html

WNAX, Radio 570, WNAX History – www.wnax.com/wnax-history/

Free Books by Charles River Editors

We have brand new titles available for free most days of the week. To see which of our titles are currently free, click on this link.

Discounted Books by Charles River Editors

We have titles at a discount price of just 99 cents everyday. To see which of our titles are currently 99 cents, click on this link.